BOLD THINKING

DIFFERENT DRUMMER

FOR THE REBELLIOUS CREATIVE

ERIK LOKKESMOE

Editorial Work: AnnaMarie McHargue

Cover Design: Aaron Snethen

Interior Design: Aaron Snethen

Photography: www.unsplash.com,
www.pexels.com

ISBN-10: 9781943425785
ISBN-13: 9781943425792

FOR THOSE WHO *MARCH*

TO THEIR OWN **BEAT.**

SOMETHIN' IN THE WATER

"Whiskey and shovels," a colleague said.

"Sorry?"

"Whiskey and shovels," he continued. "The most successful people in the Gold Rush were those who sold supplies to the miners."

The Gold Rush of 1849 was the largest migration of Americans in history. Travelers left family farms and city factories to chase rumors making their way out of the Sierra Nevada foothills.

Men (mostly), women and children came for that moment when a shovel or pan could bring instant riches. They traveled through mosquito-ravaged, rain-soaked Panama to wait (or bribe) for a boat ride up the coast to San Francisco, where crews often abandoned the boats to chase their own dreams 200 miles inland. Others took the longer, less expensive and yet more rigorous route across plains and prairies, over endless mountain ridges, abandoning worldly goods along the way to make it before the dangers of an early winter.

Charlatans, thieves, gamblers and thousands of others hoping to cash in the dream greeted the weary travelers who successfully conquered the journey. Wild rumors and selfish desires ran rampant in these river towns.

But, up the road from the chilly rivers, in the pop-up towns, were the merchants. Everyone knew that mining was only as good as the miner's tools and that survival, in its most basic form, was only as good as the flour and drink. Tools wear out. Food is required. Whiskey eases the aches of bones and the longings for home.

"Those selling whiskey and shovels were the ones who made it," the friend went on. "Most others left broke and broken-hearted."

Broke.

Broken-hearted.

Betting that *tomorrow* will be your day.

Maybe that's how you feel most days. Like your ambitions have left you standing in the cold river with an empty pan. Like your dreams will forever remain unfulfilled.

The high-flying aspirations of *what could be* are now the bedrock reality of *what is.* All around, you see others profiting and you hear others exclaim, "Eureka!"

What's your gold? What compelled you to leave everything behind, dismiss the naysayers and charlatans, to pursue something you only imagined in your mind?

For tech start-ups and indie filmmakers it may be a VC investment or a studio acquisition. Or, it may be a *People* magazine photo of a celebrity wearing your goods, or a recommendation by a Pinterest board with 1,000,000 followers.

We've all read the *Fast Company* and *Inc.* magazine stories highlighting those who have hit it big. The news both frustrates and motivates. We've paid consultants and companies, widgets and services that promised to make our way faster, smarter, more precise and more rewarding. Meanwhile, we keep digging. Business these days can feel as random as dipping your pan into the silt of a riverbank. There may be Fool's Gold, or there may be nothing. But, then, there's the slightest chance that we may find something...gold.

And that keeps us going.

Like you, I'm a prospector. For 20 years, my river has been politics and entertainment. I've been looking for the gold of voters and audiences. That's what I know best. For me, the "Eureka" moment is when distracted, mostly disinterested people do things together in a way that propels candidates to office, or movies to blockbusters.

That keeps me going.

Few industries are more demanding than politics and entertainment.

Here, you will find the most difficult—and also the most delightful—people and, at times, they are one and the same. It's a complex process with competing interests and unexpected outcomes. You could spend a year of your life giving everything you have for something you believe in, and the final night you could fail. You are competing for votes and dollars, managing large budgets and teams and, in the end, you feel it's a miracle that you even made it as far as you did.

That's the rush of the prospector. You just never know what's next. The next strike of your pick ax could forever change your destiny. It's a feeling that every entrepreneur relishes.

I grew up going to Oakland A's baseball games. "It could have been us!" is what we all yelled anytime a fan nearby caught a foul ball launched from the bats of Rickey Henderson or Dave Kingman.

"It could be us" is the driving force behind every entrepreneur—from furniture maker to filmmaker, app developer to ad agency pitching the A-list brand. It's what gets us out of bed every morning. We believe anything is possible.

And it could be you. Broke and broken-hearted doesn't need to be your destiny. Neither do flat sales or frustrated teams. This work is for those who believe in *different*. You don't believe in safe or same. You've tried doing things the way you were taught or told, and it didn't turn out the way you had hoped. Expectations are higher. Pressure is greater. Budgets are tighter. Regardless of whether you are alone or the leader of a major organization, you are that person who simply cannot shake the belief that doing the same things you've always done won't work anymore. And maybe you don't have a choice; do something different or you're out, you're closing shop, you're losing at the ballot box or the box office.

Here's the good news: It's not too late. In fact, you're early. Most are content to squeeze the blood from the turnip before things collapse. They worked for years to get to the top position. They've got big overhead. They're no longer nimble or fast. And they know it. They're just doing whatever they can to hang on. And fear drives every decision—not only fear of what's coming next quarter but fear of doing anything different.

Like you, I'm an outsider. Or I want to be. I try to be, at least. Even when I've been considered an "insider," it's never the right spot for me.

We all love the feeling of belonging. In the club. In the know. In the room. At the table. Whatever it looks like for you. The VIP status: full access, privilege and prestige.

Here's the funny thing though. The higher you climb or the closer you get, the more out of touch you become. Leveling up is more leveling out. You lose your edge. You worry too much. You realize that there is always another "inner ring." For years, I was fearful of different. I pursued the same, safe and sane life, and it was a self-inflicted curse.

Don't rock the boat. Don't ruffle anyone's feathers. Play along. Do what you are told. Speak only when spoken to. We fall in line and don't dare to march to the beat of our own drum. But the more you fit in, the more you miss out.

My career started in the most rule-intensive, insider institution on the planet. Rules for when you can speak. Rules for where you can walk. Or how you travel. Even rules for how you use the phone and your email. I was a Capitol Hill staffer, a press secretary in a Brooks Brothers suit with creative dreams beyond C-SPAN speeches or the next issue of *Roll Call* newspaper.

Rules are important. Indeed necessary. Insiders love rules. Regiments. Routines. Order and structure. Predictability and process. Chaos certainly isn't a seedbed for creativity. Every creative needs her guardrails like a locomotive needs its track. But isn't the course of human events blazed by those who refuse to play by the rules? For every rule-maker, thankfully, there's been a rule-breaker.

They're "outliers," as Malcolm Gladwell wrote. Outsiders who are restless and relentless to choose the road less traveled.

Outliers can be a problem, especially when you work in Congress. Everything is top-down, procedural and planned. The unexpected is a threat to the order of government. "Unexpected" typically means a disaster or an attack, some national calamity that puts government into a reactive mode. More proof that process and procedure are prized.

Each week on Capitol Hill, the congressional press secretaries gather to get the leadership's policy plans and talking points for the upcoming week. You were expected to follow the party line and, more importantly, to get your boss to do the same.

In all my years in Congress, I went to just *one* of those meetings. It wasn't out of arrogance or lack of interest. I didn't go because I simply believed the more expectations, the more limitations. I knew that, by going off script, I would be allowed independent thinking, fresh messaging and different takes on tough policy decisions. Government doesn't work well with disruptors. Disruption is treacherous and, if taken to the furthest degree, an act of treason.

But I knew that *different* made all the *difference*.

In fact, the "different-makers" have far more influence over people's hearts and minds than any speech or bill from Congress. I saw it firsthand. We think government has the power, but as a few friends would say, politics is downstream from the artist. Here's the thesis: The creative will do more to shape the direction of culture than the White House or U.S. Senate. Way upstream in the formation of culture and ideas and beliefs is the creative—the rule-breaker, the misfit, the outsider.

Stories and songs and social good start-ups shape the imagination. Government has the power to enforce; the artist has the power to entice. "Imagination rules the world," wrote Napoleon; or as one philosopher, a contemporary of Plato, stated, "Give me the songs of the nation and I care not who writes its laws." Consider an AMC TV series or a Paramount blockbuster film, Billboard's Top 100, the latest book from Simon & Schuster, *Vogue* magazine, the hottest iTunes app, or the new Kenneth Cole ad along Henry Hudson Parkway in New York City—these are informing beliefs and behaviors far more than the next Senate bill or CNN presidential debate.

Historically, artists always have been outsiders. The outcasts don't fight to get inside the power systems—they ignore them altogether. The old kingdom is collapsing from within by those who stand outside the city gates. Each week a few dozen of us met regularly inside the halls of Congress to remind artists and writers and filmmakers and authors to keep going. Tom Wolfe. Bono. Patricia Heaton. The Fray. We'd remind them: Don't look to us to change things. Government is the reservoir at the end of the cultural river. You, as creatives, are the tributaries. What you do can change a generation in an instant (consider 1,000,000,000 views of Adele's song, "Hello") or a generation from now.

In 1995 I spent a summer as a river guide on the American River in the foothills of the Sierra mountains, floating by the very banks where tens of thousands of miners worked 150 years earlier. Gold Rush history is still visible along the river, whether through old timers still sifting the sand or where water canons blasted away mountainsides and changed the course of the river.

In so many ways, American "culture," our nation's social ecosystem, resembles that river. Is there any doubt that the river is flowing at full force with Class V rapids created by steep gradients, constricted flow and El Niño-type flash floods? It twists and turns, drops and churns, erodes banks and erases anything that stands in its way. The entirety of media and entertainment, politics and education, business and health care, journalism and global affairs is raging in the river, and the water is rising.

Some, whooping and hollering with no clue what's ahead, are joyriding down the river in a raft filled with a keg of beer, drifting wherever the current takes them. Others are avoiding the river altogether, afraid to go near its power. Certainly there are those who are trying to dam (or, is it "damn?") the river, stop its flow in the name of tradition, politics or religion.

And, then, there are others who are at the source of the river—they are the small streams, the tributaries, and springs that are creating the flow—these are the artists, the creative, the difference-makers, the outcasts, the rebels who believe that what they start there can shape lives for better or for worse, even for those way down at the end of the river.

This guide is designed to be your guide. I'm someone who has been in the raft 20 years, and there's no question that I've learned more what NOT to do than what to do. This booklet reflects my doubts and dreams, lessons and longings. It's about the source. About the river. About the gold that still needs to be found, if only we keep dreaming dreams and sharing visions. And, it's about that bedrock belief that though the river rages through beauty and brokenness, it still flows through Sovereign land. All of it, I believe, is the Creator's. We are here to steward the river, and that begins with seeing everything differently.

I'm asked from time to time how I jumped out of politics into entertainment. The answer is, "I have absolutely no clue." Seriously. All I can say is that entertainment is political and politics is entertaining. The two worlds are more sisters than warring neighbors. Of course, I had a few friends in the movie business who asked me, a restless outsider, to do things no one else would dare try. They had me at "hello."

It was 2006. Things were changing faster than anyone had anticipated, especially in entertainment. Content was getting smaller and smarter, thanks to changes in digital filmmaking. Distribution was breaking up. Technology, especially social media, was moving out of the dorm rooms into the boardrooms. Audiences wanted more than mere enjoyment; they wanted to participate, to "enter" into entertainment.

The entire entertainment apparatus was built upon a system of protectionism. A command-central mentality that everything must be controlled, calculated, centralized. And yet, everything outside of Hollywood was democratizing, decentralizing, disrupting.

"Hollywood," in short, was becoming a *term* more than a *town*.

The executives who had worked for 15 years to earn that corner suite and the Brioni suit now faced empty cubicles and shortfalls in revenue. The models they learned, the strategies they perfected, the thinking they adopted—all had changed. Nothing was going to work like it used to and, as a result, from president to production assistant, everything became about self-preservation.

The old saying that "you are only as good as your last project" took on new power. Doing the same old thing won't raise eyebrows, but it won't raise any celebratory champagne glasses either. The executive's dilemma is real: Innovate and you are in jeopardy of being blamed if it goes south; don't innovate and you risk being overlooked and deemed irrelevant.

As Thoreau wrote, we should always remember, "the duty, inconvenience and dangers of conformity, in little things and great."

Hollywood is built upon a system of conformity; and yet, conformity is the very reason it's struggling.

In the early part of 2008, I decided to risk everything to be an outsider once again. As I told my wife, "My arm is getting tired from throwing caution to the wind." And, yet, we set out to start a marketing company that was truly different.

If you are going to leave a company, marketing books advise do so only when you have secured a few clients to come along with you. That wasn't an option, so we did the next best thing: We started a company that confirmed the fears of prospective clients. It was no lie—everything was changing and nothing would work like it used to. The studios knew it. We were just surfacing their fears.

Over the past eight years, we've had the privilege of sitting at the table with executives of the best and biggest content creators on the planet. We've been amazed at the level of creativity and innovation, the experience and commitment, the goodwill and generosity of so many. And, we've been given the chance—faster than most—to work on projects that have reordered how entertainment is created, distributed, marketed and consumed.

We had no intention of creating a company that did what everyone else did—but with just a bit more tenacity or a slightly lower fee. That is the old way. Our goal was not to change Hollywood, an impossible task. Instead, we set out to earn the right to show a different way of marketing...and, over time, see these new tactics become standard in the industry...and, as a result, to *turn* Hollywood.

Without question, despite the massive budgets (of which we were decimal dust) and entrenched strategies (over which we actually had some say) we've turned the industry toward a more decentralized, democratized approach to reach audiences.

It works because we've had this healthy balance of loving the industry and loving the audience—insiders with an outsider perspective; outsiders with insider experience.

We knew enough to be dangerous but not enough to be declawed.

Lasting change happens from the inside out, the bottom-up, and rarely from the outside in or the top-down. A failing public school in Portland didn't change until a group of churchgoers started serving the school unconditionally with clean up days, spaghetti feeds, day care service and coat closets. It wasn't a city council asking, "What do they need?" that changed things; change happened when people started loving students and teachers with the simple question, "How can we help?"

Bottom-up. Inside out.

I've often said that our clients hire us, in part, because we know what *to* do, and, in part, because we know what *not* to do. Opportunity gives you zeal. Experience gives you perspective.

Not that long ago, I decided that the lessons we've learned in the trenches were unique to us but not unique to our industry; these lessons had to be shared. These lessons could not and should not be held close to the vest. We are all prospectors. What worked for movies and TV shows, books and music could also, we discovered, be applied to health care and insurance, retail and restaurants.

We all live in the most cluttered marketplace in history, as Seth Godin rightly says. An audience that pays attention is essential to get an audience that pays at all. But how?

A friend says that "awareness" is a 90's word; the word of today is "action," getting people to do something, to put their hand on it and make it move. To participate, that is gold for us marketers. To be loyal and life-long consumers for brands and products. To get people to do something that matters.

A youth leader told me that if she organized a miniature golf night, a fair share of students would show up. If she planned a night of distributing blankets to the homeless, however, the number would swell to double its expected size. The rising generations don't want to be entertained; they are unwilling to ask permission. Their DNA is crackling with what's possible in a broken world passed down by their elders.

The Hollywood production company, Participant Media, built its entire culture and projects around a simple, yet compelling idea: TakePart. Passive observers are scandalized, but participants are idolized.

We are all participants now, all outsiders.

No one has mastered marketing. Everyone is learning in real time. As the New Balance ad reads: Always In Beta. In other words, always refining and reworking, never finished. Some are mastering the market faster than others. No question, it's tough out there. Still, some offer whiskey and shovels, and surely everyone needs some courage and tools. This is a guide for the rest of us. We are the dreamers and doers. We've made the sacrifice. We've taken the risks. Now let's reap the rewards.

It is time to share what we've learned in acquiring, activating and accelerating an audience with those who are trying to reach consumers or donors or voters—whether to market a bar of soap, a film, a car, a candidate or a cause. We offer musings and mistakes and Eureka moments, knowing that our ideas and offerings may make sense for you—no matter your place in life or work or belief. We hold these as our own "self-evident truths," and welcome rolled-eyes and angry social posts on Facebook as much as we welcome high-fives and heads tired from nodding so often.

If there's one lesson learned, and one that we hope you learn from us, it's this:

Different has been, and always will be, the differentiator between individuals, ideas and industries.

A small twist.

A unique perspective.

An unconventional approach.

A different take.

As we say in our office, "Never the same." It's nothing new, really. We all grew up with the Apple ad from 1997 that put into words the restlessness of our spirits:

Here's to the crazy ones. The misfits. The rebels. The troublemakers. The round pegs in the square holes. The ones who see things differently. They're not fond of rules. And they have no respect for the status quo. You can quote them, disagree with them, glorify or vilify them. About the only thing you can't do is ignore them. Because they change things. They push the human race forward. And while some may see them as the crazy ones, we see genius. Because the people who are crazy enough to think they can change the world, are the ones who do.

Makers may make, but marketers make it known. We criticize by creating. We see things others don't. We play an essential role, now more than ever. We are the crazy ones, the outsiders, the kids who are not let into the circle. We are different, and that is a good thing.

The river is flowing. The guide is ready. Let's launch.

—Erik Lokkesmoe

- ENTERTAINMENT -

WHY ENTERTAINMENT?

"Why do you work in entertainment?" I was asked one day. A good question. An hour later, long after the conversation ended, I had my answer: To "build soil," which is a line from a Robert Frost poem. To create an environment where life takes root. To plow your yield back into the ground means that you don't do it for money or credits—money goes away, credits fade. The only purpose is to help the storyteller and the story hearer flourish—and so we need to "build soil" in a parched landscape.

IS CONTENT KING?

Twelve thousand movies are submitted to Sundance a year; 120 get in. A handful will get deals. More and more content being made, more and more audiences segmented. More and more platforms than ever. Fewer and fewer distributors. So, is CONTENT still king? Or does the AUDIENCE now occupy the throne?

WHAT DO YOU WANT FROM YOUR AUDIENCE?

Do you want your audience to:

Sit back in their seat?

Hold on to their seat?

Lean forward in their seat?

It's not enough anymore just to think about filling seats.

YOUR FILM

"Prove it or lose it"—how movie theaters treat your film
"Spray and pray"—how marketers treat your film
"Stay (home) or go"—how audiences treat your film
"One and done"—how studios treat indie filmmakers

HALF-HEARTED CONSUMERS

Author C.S. Lewis, in his *The Weight of Glory*, wrote, "We are halfhearted creatures. We are fooling about with drink and sex and ambition when infinite joy is offered us, like an ignorant child who wants to go on making mud pies in a slum because he cannot imagine what is meant by the offer of a holiday at the sea. We are far too easily pleased."

We are far too easily pleased with the current state of art and entertainment. Francis Schaeffer rightly proclaimed that the imagination should fly beyond the stars—and, yet, too often, our imaginations resemble a moth circling a cabin light. We are half-hearted creatures, prone to pick the dry and plain, the safe and soggy.

MORE CONVERSATION

A college professor asked me a question about the differences between religious films that target the Church, target mass market, or target the indie audience. Think *God's Not Dead, Son of God, Noah Exodus,* and *Calvary The Tree of Life.* My answer was: The first are about confirmation of beliefs, the second are about commercialization of beliefs, the last are about conversation around beliefs. The latter is the future.

WHAT BAD CHRISTIAN MOVIES TEACH HOLLYWOOD

For a Hollywood executive, popularity and profit are the primary measures of success—the only things that matter. So when a religious movie with bad theology and production quality makes $60,000,000 at the box office, what's the executive's response?

Oh, wait, so you mean this audience wants bad stories with bad acting and production, made for no money and marketed just to them? Heck, we can do that!

There is a song from the 70s with the lyrics, "They will know we are Christians by our love." Today we could change the lyrics to be: "They will know we are Christians by our low-production movies."

We hear a lot of talk that we now live in a post-Christian world—that America's general consensus around ethics and law, entertainment and health, church and civil society is no longer predominately Christian.

This has caused many Christians to feel anxious or anger, which often manifests in an expression of fight or flight. Either to take the country back or start building the backyard bunker and stock it with canned beans.

There's another option, however. What if we saw the culture as pre-Christian—that we refresh the page and see what is possible? What if we rush in, be present and faithful, love until it breaks us and see everything as a possibility? Only with that posture can we ask new questions, tell new stories. Only then can we really engage those unlike us. Be attentive to what is around us; authentic in how we live and honest about who we really are.

—

BAD MOVIES ALWAYS LIE. THEY LIE MOST OF ALL ABOUT THE HUMAN CONDITION.
— PARAPHRASING WALKER PERCY; STEVEN GARBER'S VISIONS OF VOCATION

—

EVERYTHING ELSE IS A BRAND DEPOSIT

The unforeseen consequence of big blockbusters like *Jurassic World* on indie films:

"...what used to be the backbone of Hollywood movie making, namely self-contained, non-repeatable scripts, now threatens to become an anomaly, a charity act, a niche, a tithe to awards season, or a skippable option?...It's one that is imperiled by a movie universe in which studios are increasingly defined by their ability to maximize three or four major properties per year with almost everything else being a nonfactor." – *Grantland.com*

THE ART OF PUNCTUATION

One way to view films is through punctuation. Yes, seriously. Here's how:

Some films are exclamation points (!), high-energy, emphatic or ideological.

Others films are dot, dot, dot—ellipsis (...), giving the audience pause, silence or a sense that things are to be continued.

Still others are periods (.), offering complete thoughts, with little room for discussion or disagreement.

But maybe the best films are the question marks (?), raising big questions and ideas, letting the audiences come to their own conclusions and allowing mystery and ambiguity to give tension and attention to the story.

ANOTHER WAY TO RATE CONTENT

One way to rate movies and television is not thumbs up or down, stars or numbers. Rather, base it on what drink pairs best with the story and it says a lot. Wine means relaxing and refined. Beer means gritty and robust. Whiskey means strong and hard-hitting. Lemonade is playful and great for the family.

HEAD. HEART. HAND.

What kind of films do we love? Here's one way to say it, paraphrasing St. Francis: He who works with his hands is a laborer. He who works with his hands and his head is a craftsman. He who works with his hands and his head and his heart is an artist. So, short answer, we love films that connect head, heart and soul made by the hands of great talent.

A LITTLE GRIT

Some of the best films are like jumping on a Slip 'N Slide on a gravel road; you feel everything, you'll never forget it, and you'll tell everyone you know about the experience!

SMART FILMS FOR SOULFUL PEOPLE

A great film has a heart (inspiration) and mind (cognition) and soul (aspiration) and perspiration (action) for what is true, good and beautiful

CUT-AND- / PASTE CREATIVITY

Entertainment and media have the appearance of innovation, but, at their core, these creative industries are mostly driven by a copycat, audience chasing, assembly line, throw-anything-against-the-wall approach. Perpetual disruption of models and endless questioning of assumptions are required to win. Tear up the playbook, folks.

DOODLING

HAPPENS IN THE MARGINS

Great films gift to the audience the necessary margins to experience, explore and express what is and what could be—the time and space for them to come to their own conclusions and start their own conversations. Too many "films" (no need to mention them here) are fearful of the margins and leave no room for ambiguity. You are told what to feel, what to think, and what to believe. That is propaganda, not art.

THE MIDDLE IS GONE

The gap between big and small entertainment is widening. Mid-sized content is going, going, gone. If you are aiming for the middle, don't. Aim small. Miss small.

IN THE ROOM

We've made it easier and even more lucrative to remain on the fringes of entertainment and media than it is to be in the room, in the middle, in the heart of the industry where real impact happens behind (and beyond) the screen.

BE LIKEABLE

If you want a shot in Hollywood, here are some basic rules that you may want to put into practice:

1. Pay your bills, especially to your vendors.
2. Keep your word.
3. Be likeable.
4. Give others credit.
5. Be kind to the assistants.
6. Don't use people.
7. Be tenacious.
8. Be really good at what you do.
9. Stick around long enough.
10. Love the industry.

D IS FOR...

Disruption

Democratization

Data

Distribution

Denial

Five words that describe what's trending—or will be—in Hollywood.

A MOVIE WON'T CHANGE HOLLYWOOD

If you want a strategy to improve Hollywood, here it is: Send 5,000 exceptionally talented, tenacious and trained creative people into the industry to spend the next 20 years offering a better way, starting at the bottom and daily earning the right and respect to lead.

THE BIG MELTDOWN

Steven Spielberg said, "That's the big danger, and there's eventually going to be an implosion—or a big meltdown. There's going to be an implosion where three or four or maybe even a half-dozen mega-budget movies are going to go crashing into the ground, and that's going to change the paradigm."

Seems there is another kind of "implosion" happening— an insecure (on every level) industry, an isolated industry, and an intimidated industry. This is not going away. Implosions are going to be a regular thing.

-POLITICS-

THE HOLLYWOOD FOR UGLY PEOPLE

Politics is entertaining and, more often than we realize, entertainment is political.

—

WHAT HAPPENS "INSIDE THE BELTWAY" AND WHAT HAPPENS "INSIDE THE STUDIO" ARE SURPRISINGLY SIMILAR. DROP A CAPITOL HILL STAFFER INTO A HOLLYWOOD CONFERENCE ROOM AND HE WOULD FIND THE ROOM REMARKABLY FAMILIAR, JUST WITHOUT THE BROOKS BROTHERS SUITS AND STIFF FORMALITY. THE TALK WOULD BE OF CAMPAIGNS, TRACKING, TARGET AUDIENCE, MEDIA SPENDS, MESSAGING AND FIELD STAFF.

—

MR. SMITH GOES TO HOLLYWOOD

It's said that every political press secretary has a movie screenplay in his desk drawer. Maybe it's time for every Hollywood marketing executive to keep a *Roll Call* newspaper in his.

FAILING UP

In Hollywood, as it is in politics, executives fail up.

THREE THINGS YOU RARELY HEAR IN POLITICS

To an opponent,
 "That's a good point."
To the press,
 "I don't know."
To the voters, before getting caught,
 "I was wrong."

—

HUMILITY IS WRONGLY PERCEIVED AS
A SELF-INFLICTED WOUND IN POLITICS.

—

INDEPENDENT DEPENDENCY

It's a lost cause for conservatives until someone articulates the balance of a government that you can depend on without having a government that you are dependent on.

KEEP 'EM GUESSING

In politics, we must put principle before party. No party deserves our loyalty or our love. Our politics should undoubtedly surprise others and, at times, ourselves. The goal may simply be: Be more conservative than any conservative and more liberal than any liberal.

THE ART OF THE POSSIBLE

Politics may be the art of the possible, but art might not be possible in politics. Politics has an end in mind. Art is ambiguity. Start mixing the two and, at best, you atrophy your imagination muscle and, at worst, you create art that distrusts the audience, leaving no margin for questions or conversations.

THE PAINTER OF SHADOWS

How does a sanitized view of entertainment and art affect us? First, it discourages our artists from exploring and exposing the bad, the lies and the ugliness of our world.

"A painter uses both light and shadows in her work," preacher Billy Graham said. Profoundly true. If a painter did not use shadows, the page would be a line drawing with no depth or texture. The light doesn't stand out as much.

Many creatives, especially in Hollywood, have let their eyes adjust too much to the darkness—they are used to the dark and see no reason to lighten the room.

Others have overexposed the art. Think about photographers in a dark room. They are in the dark room because too much light would blanche the image. Too much light ruins it.

Is it possible to have too much light?

As broken people we are prone to overexpose, to rush people headlong into change, to find their road to Damascus experience, to create a big neon arrow sign just in case anyone misses it.

Yes, we can absolutely flood art with too much light.

And, as a result, it disregards and distrusts the audience.

ART HURTS

One of the primary roles of art—whether popular or classic—is to comfort the afflicted and afflict the comfortable. Art is designed to disrupt, challenge. It must be fearless. It must be a resistance. Artists literally draw the line. Hollywood is as cowardly as D.C., no surprise there.

SOMETHING PERMANENT

"The root meaning of the Latin and Greek words translated as 'rule' is trellis," writes the author of *Benedict's Dharma*. The trellis is the structure that supports the growth of vines and plants. There are things that cannot grow without fixed and permanent and sturdy apparatus to latch onto or wrap around. The same is true in creativity—we need institutions and structures that allow the artists (filmmakers, poets, architects, furniture makers, etc.) to have stability and strength. Increasingly, I'm concerned that we are not building enough of these—and are trying to grow things without these important frames. We need long-standing, long-term, deep foundational structures around arts and entertainment that allow the artist and the audience to flourish.

DO YOU PREFER STORIES THAT SHOW THE WORLD AS...

It is?
It could be?
It should be?
As it was?

- MARKETING -

MARKETING IS ABOUT AUDIENCE

Successful distribution is 10 percent mechanics and 90 percent marketing. Audience. Audience. Audience. You can say story is king, but the audience holds the keys and the sword.

NARROW IS THE ROAD

Marketing used to be about how to expand your audience. Marketing today must be about how to compress your audience. Intensity is everything.

WHAT DO YOU WANT FOR YOUR AUDIENCE?

When marketing entertainment (or politics or causes or products), instead of asking what you want FROM an audience, you should be asking what you want FOR an audience. The moment you see individuals only as ticket sales (or votes or donations or money), well, then it's time for you to leave the business.

You should be asking yourself and your team: How do we become the company that puts us out of business?

— Danny Meyer, CEO

CHUM IN THE WATER

Old marketing is about pushing, the "throw-everything-at-them" strategy of saturation.

New marketing is about pulling, the "come-see-what-I've-got" strategy of enticement.

A THEOLOGY OF MARKETING

Want a theology of marketing? First principle: Love your audience. Second: Don't create discontentment. Third: Shut down on the Sabbath. Fourth: Concede that excellence brings influence. Fifth: Ask questions and create conversations. What would you add?

BALLOT BOX OFFICE

Political campaigns have one objective—get millions of people to do one thing on a single day: cast a vote. Entertainment campaigns have one objective, too—get millions of people to do one thing on a single weekend: buy a ticket. That may sound simplistic, a whitewashing of any complex differences such as the size of budgets, the role of celebrities or the intense passions around divisive issues. (For those political folks who think movie marketing doesn't have challenges like those of a campaign, consider the clutter and competition to motivate people with 1,000 other choices to leave their house, get a sitter, park, spend $12 a ticket and risk leaving disappointed.) Nevertheless, all the obvious differences aside, if you strip away everything else, what remains is this: both must get busy, distracted people to do something together, en masse, at the same time in a way that doesn't directly or immediately benefit themselves.

SPRAY AND PRAY

Marketing, traditionally and generally speaking, is about awareness and impressions. It's about going after as many people as possible and trying to convince enough to actually do what you want them to do. In entertainment, it's mass marketing—an inch deep, but a mile wide in its strategy. All essential, of course, but Excedrin moments begin when you consider obvious trends. The splintering of audiences. The proliferation of digital. The rise of Netflix over conventional television viewing. The numbers of readers and viewers is declining among traditional outlets. Once invincible and profitable powerhouse media outlets are freefalling (*Newsweek* sold for $1!) Marketing, as a result, naturally becomes specialized, niche, surgical. More scalpel than chainsaw. Still, especially in entertainment marketing, even the best marketers are left to attempt more and more on fewer and fewer dollars. The strategy ends up looking something like this: Try everything, hope for something; and this: Check the boxes, don't do anything risky. In the end, millions of impressions with not that many results.

WALK PRECINCTS NOT RED CARPETS

Entertainment marketers should spend a summer as a Senate press aide or on the campaign trail in rural Georgia. Sure, it would be a 90 percent pay cut, but the lessons would be faster than earning a degree from George Washington University. Most instructional would be the discovery that there is a big difference between marketing and mobilizing, and how both are needed to win in the most cluttered entertainment marketplace in history.

—

THE MAKERS MAY DO THE MAKING, BUT IT'S THE MARKETERS WHO MAKE IT KNOWN.

—

TWO CANDIDATES WALK INTO AN INTERVIEW

Two candidates for a marketing job stand before you. One tells you what works in marketing. The other tells you what doesn't work. Who do you hire?

WHAT'S MISSING?

The former chairman of the National Endowment took visitors to the National Gallery of Art. This was a special treat as he was one of the top five Renaissance art historians in the world. It would have been odd for him to tell of the greatness of a Raphael painting or a Lombardo sculpture by what the artist did NOT include. Right? It would be weird if we determined good art by what is not there. Well, then, why do some critics determine that a film or book or song is good simply because it does not have violence, language, sexual situations or mature themes? It's good if it's good, not because of what is missing.

MADE
YOU
LOOK

The intent of advertising used to be: make you look. Then it was: make you feel. Today, advertising is: make you look at others and feel discontented.

DON'T GIVE THEM WHAT THEY ASK FOR

If you are a marketer, you either can deliver what the client wants, or you can deliver what the client needs. The former is about doing what it takes to make a dollar. The latter is about doing what it takes to make a difference... and, lo and behold, by doing so, you get better clients and better money.

MAKE THEM PICKY

Marketing is primarily about one thing: making consumers picky about what they consume.

—

SOCIAL MEDIA MAY JUST BE OUR ATTEMPT TO HAVE SOCIAL MEANING.

—

WHY EVERYONE HAS A MOBILE PHONE ON THE DINNER TABLE

For my parents' and grandparents' generations, media is a diversion.

For the millennial generation, media is digestion, a natural part of life.

WEBSITES ARE COUNTRY CLUBS

Websites are like billboards. Or maybe it's more like a country club on the outskirts of town. People know it's there. They are glad it's there. They may even visit once in a while. But, it's mostly old people who come for the predictable offerings. And, members have no idea that there is a raging social party happening down the street at the community pool.

DATA? I DON'T NEED NO STINKIN' DATA

Few would dispute that the creative industries are ahead of politics in everything from technology to inspiring audiences. Yet, there are a number of ways D.C. is way ahead of Hollywood. When a top television executive toured a national political campaign headquarters to see its massive database and social tracking operation, she was blown away and remarked that she had "never seen anything like this." It's true; politics' voter list acquisition, targeting and mobilization strategies are a decade ahead of anything used by marketers in entertainment. To that point, a movie-marketing executive recently pondered aloud, "Data? Why would I want data?"

THE CAR ALARM IN THE MALL PARKING LOT

Awareness is a 90's word. Action is the word of today. Yes, awareness is essential. People cannot act upon something they don't even know about. The assumption of yesterday was that awareness was enough. Not so in a world of 500 television channels, one billion YouTube videos and a new blog created every few seconds. Awareness is just another car alarm in a mall parking lot—it makes a lot of noise, but no one pays any attention.

OK, ALL TOGETHER NOW

Mobilization is the tidal wave of the future. At its core, mobilization is about identifying, activating and accelerating a particular audience, and then intensifying its participation and "ownership" toward a specific day or ask. Easy enough, right? Wrong. High-touch segmentation down to single influencers. Online and offline blending. Customization on crack. This is where blue-collar meets blue ocean—hard work and big ideas.

THE FUNNEL

If marketing was defined by a shape, it would be an arrow. Obvious, directional, no ambiguity. You see it. You may follow. You may act. Mobilization, in comparison, would be a funnel. Intensifying as it moves you toward a specific direction.

PUT ME IN, COACH

Mobilization is defined by "action," measurable acts that create participation from the earliest point all the way to the very end. Audiences want to do more than "buy a ticket"; they want to be participants. Research shows that if you can get someone to do one thing now, they are far more likely to do more in the future.

INTENTIONAL RANDOMNESS

When mobilization works, it may appear as an unexpected random convergence of fans, when in reality it's a highly orchestrated, strategic coordination designed and executed behind the scenes.

THE ROAR OF THE PROUD

Marketing is a monologue with consumers; mobilization, however, is a packed arena of fans chanting in unison, starting with a few and growing in size and volume.

BOREDOM IN THE BOARDROOM

If you are someone with a movie—whether studio or indie—who is looking for marketing, ask the agency or consultant how they will prove that what they did sold tickets, and didn't just do a bunch of activity that may look good in a report, but was a waste of resources.

Here's the problem with most marketing today. It's boring. Look at some of these movie campaigns: heavy, serious, important. "Eat your peas, audience!" Bleh! Have some fun! Do things that cause heads to turn, eyes to roll or hearts to skip a beat—the stuff that shows signs of life. One reason things aren't working is because your work has no personality.

THE WAIT IS OVER

The "boredom economy" will only keep booming as companies and creators capitalize on consumer downtime through mobile games, ebooks, short films, apps, music and so on. Subway rides, stuck in traffic, shopping lines, car trips, airplanes, waiting for someone at a restaurant... the days of "patiently doing nothing" are over.

LIVING UPSIDE DOWN

In politics, in art and entertainment, in education, in every field we pursue, in every part of our lives...we are called to upside-down lives.

It means living a life that astonishes people—one that is so subversive, so surprisingly counter-cultural and counter-intuitive that it causes people to shake their heads in disbelief—and in wonder.

SPEND TIME IN THE LIBRARY CHILDREN'S SECTION

Three styles of children's books should be models for marketers:

1. Connect the dots
2. Pull, flip, lift; interactive books
3. Mad Libs

Do you know why?

—

OWN THE AUDIENCE, THEN YOU'LL OWN THE CONTENT.

—

YOUR COMPETITION IS THE CLUTTER

For movie marketers, you're not competing against other movies opening the same weekend. You are competing against the 10,000 other options consumers have to entertain themselves or spend their money. If I were a movie theater chain, or even a studio, I'd be advertising why going to the movies is the best choice over all other options. A consumer that "waits" is a significant threat to exhibitors. That's why creating great theatrical experiences is so important.

IT'S ALL PERSONAL

In the past, people looked to military leaders, presidents and scientists for answers. Today, people look to creatives for answers.

In the past, people looked for evidence, for logic and reasoned arguments. Today, people look for ambiguity, narrative and questions.

In the past, people found meaning and significance within the larger community. Today, people find meaning and significance within their own self-created communities.

DON'T FEAR DIFFICULTY

Here's what I've realized after nine years in movie marketing...there are two types of movies that call on my
company for help: those that are difficult to market, and
those that fall into the in-between space. How fitting,
since those are the movies that I love to work on anyhow.
Smart, entertaining films for soulful people who care
about real things. If that's my life's work, fine by me.

LESSONS LEARNED

Know your audience.

Create a consistent, compelling and coordinated campaign strategy. Don't just throw $hit against the wall—create a plan and stick to it.

Break every rule. If you are doing something "traditional," stop, and rethink every assumption.

Don't exaggerate your momentum. You're likely not doing nearly as well as you think.

Data. Data. Data. Do everything you can to collect real-time data, analytics, measurable, tracking and audience information.

Eventize. Eventize. Eventize. No, it's not a "real" word but it's a real strategy. Your marketing must create moments. Moments typically are born out of experiences and events.

TOP-DOWN VS. BOTTOM-UP

Top-down marketing doesn't guarantee success. Your strategy must be street-level, bottom-up. In other words, just because some well-known personality supports your product doesn't mean that his or her followers will do the same.

FURTHER UP, FURTHER IN

"Aspiration" is healthy rebellion against the way things are or the way things "have to be." Aspirational brands get Maslow's hierarchy of need and integrate their marketing around moving people higher—not lower.

REACH LOW

Have low-shelf calls to action. Never leave a screening without giving definitive, clear, actionable asks from the audience. Requesting their email or a Facebook "like" is not a call to action.

MORE LESSONS LEARNED

Don't chase the approval of elites or industries. Your goal is to find your audience and make money. Do that, and you will get their attention and approval.

Most word of mouth still happens offline. Make sure your marketing has a good blend of online and offline strategies.

People are your best investment. Hire good people in your target markets and audiences to personalize your product and create "ownership."

Publicity doesn't mean as much as you think it does. The goal for your film is not publicity; the goal is ubiquity.

Thank those who help you. Gratitude goes a long way in an industry that is all about who takes the credit.

Create ways for your audience to participate in the success of your product. Don't make it all about "buying." Invite audiences to join in every step of the way.

Don't run from controversy. All press is good press.

Build broad, diverse "coalitions" of audiences. Every creative work should have at least dozens of significant marketing partners behind it, such as charities, associations and tastemakers.

Think twice before putting a publicist on retainer.

Audiences are fickle. Don't assume people will show up.

Long-lead marketing is essential. Don't rush. You need at least six months to acquire, activate and accelerate your audience.

Hope is not a strategy.

Don't spend too long marketing your film or book or music. You will burn out your most important supporters. Create a plan. Pick a date. Then move on to your next project.

USING PEOPLE

In marketing, you can either use people to promote your product or you can use your product to promote people.

GO FAST OR GO FAR

"If you want to go fast, go alone. If you want to go far, go together," says the African proverb. Who is with you for the long haul?

IS IT A MOVEMENT?

"How do you define if something is a movement? Good question. I do really believe history determines it. And if you say that word, you are likely trying to get someone's attention, money and friends. Look, imagine if you are a mad artist working on a painting. If you are any good at your art, you would never step back and say, 'This is a masterpiece,' before it is done. Very few artists—if they are good ones—finish a painting and self-declare it a masterpiece. It requires someone else to say that. To have a different perspective after some time has passed. So, to say, 'I am working on something and it is a movement' is like saying I am an artist working on a painting and it is a masterpiece. But, saying it's a movement is great marketing. People love to be a part of movements."

– Justin Dillon, musician and social entrepreneur

WELCOME THE CRAZY

The upside-down, bottom-up, top-down, inside-out, outside-in, topsy-turvy, head-snapping, head-shaking, back-breaking, heart-pounding, hand-wringing, (did I say back-breaking?), rule-bending state of marketing is here to stay. If I have any advice for marketing, it's to have an exceptional product, backed by exceptional people, who have an exceptional amount of persistence and patience.

ADVICE FOR
- CREATIVES -

FOMO AND ICYMI

Two interesting social dynamics are happening: FOMO (fear of missing out) and ICYMI (in case you missed it). The former is happening to consumers. The latter is happening to creators. One has to be in the know. The other is trying to get known. Both are a result of the speed and endless flow of content today. The goal: to be okay with missing out. And to create timeless, compelling content that endures.

WELL, THIS SHOULD BE INTERESTING

"Certain new realities are beyond argument: Clutter is up—more ads, more channels, more content—advertising rates continue to drop, and audiences are programming their own universe in text, video and audio. Consumers don't want to watch commercials, are fleeing networks, hate reruns, are increasingly bored by reality programming, shun print products and, oh, by the way, don't want to pay much for content either."

– *The New York Times*

"M" IS FOR...

Margins
Meaning
Musings
Mystery

Four things that great art gives its audience.
What would you add?

THE FIXERS

Many of us have this natural inclination, born out of our joy and hope, to fix things. We are all a mess—even if no one admits it—and yet we don't like messiness. Artists are messy. They wear their brokenness on the outside, while the rest of us try to cram it down into dark places where no one will ever discover it.

WHERE'S THE KICK?

The world is suspicious of crisp and clean, no-caffeine creativity.

MY AGENDA IS
NOT TO HAVE ONE

Great art begins and ends with mystery, a question, an unexpected outcome. Madeleine L'Engle, the author of *A Wrinkle in Time* and other classic works like, *Walking on Water*—who passed away recently—describes this idea of an artist entering into their work—a blank canvas, a blank screen, a blank page—with no certainty of what will be on the other side. She describes how, during one of her stories, a character suddenly appeared—a character she had never introduced or imagined—he was just there in the room, and she went with it.

BONO FOR PRESIDENT

The most influential force in our culture is not the politician, nor is it the senator or even the president. It is the artist. Napoleon said, "Imagination rules the world!" It is true: The artists—the poets, the musicians, the actors, the fashion designers—they shape the hearts and minds of the world, for better or for worse. An ancient philosopher said, "Give me the songs of the nation and I care not who writes its laws." Most can recite every word of a U2 song from 20 years ago, but very few could tell you one bill the current president signed into law.

THE MISSING MIDDLE

War-torn countries have "no-fly zones," areas that are off-limits to both sides. Culture wars have the same thing. But let me ask you: Will you live and love in that middle space, the no-fly zones of our culture? That is where we are called to be, in the streets, on a hillside, along the shoreline. The middle space doesn't mean abandoning your convictions; it doesn't mean voting independent or sprinkling a few swear words into your conversations. It is more radical than that; it is about dwelling in the beautiful mess. The middle space is a lonely place. But it's the only space that crackles with electricity from the mix of people and possibilities.

10TH ROW, CENTER SEAT

If we really want to shape the future, we must be in the center of cultural influence, and that happens inside the creative industries. On Broadway stages. In newsrooms. On studio lots. In recording studios. Otherwise we are nothing more than commentators and critics.

SERVING COFFEE TO EXECUTIVES

The only way to influence society is to be fully present. Real transformation never happens from a safe distance. The culture is messy, filled with broken people—like us. A missionary to China said years ago, "Some people want to work within the sound of church or chapel bell—I want to work within a yard of hell." Real transformation is never from the top-down, the outside in. To change it, you have to first work as a mailroom clerk at Paramount Studios. You have to intern at Capitol Music Group. You have to handle customer complaints at Apple.

You have to work your way up.

CHECK YOUR ALIGNMENT

Make sure everyone on your project is aligned with the desired goals and outcomes, and, then, structure a relationship that is meaningful but flexible.

THE MAGIC OF LIKE-MINDEDNESS

That feeling in the room when you're with professionals who are exceptionally talented with real-world credentials and share your aspiration. Yeah, that's magical.

—

"BE A PERSON OF IMPACT AND INFLUENCE WITHOUT NEEDING TO BE A PERSON OF IMPACT AND INFLUENCE."
—SCOTTY SMITH, AUTHOR

—

THE WHISPER CAMPAIGN

There's nothing wrong with "loud" change, meaning big and consequential events that turn heads and hearts. Election days and Supreme Court decisions, huge ratings for television series and so on. We are all drawn to the moments that are measurable—with clear winners and losers. "Quiet" change, however, is far more consequential. Small and simple, when no one is keeping score and when most will never know or care. We should gladly take a million of those over a dozen "loud" victories.

MONEY ISN'T THE MOTIVATION

Making a lot of money has never been the motivation. There are plenty of ways to do that, especially in my industry. It's always been about a different path, a more difficult road—to put our hands on the content and companies that will leave an indelible imprint on people and society. To do those things that, when you sit down with your partners, raise your glass and say, "I cannot believe we got to do that. Look what we did together." If that's the end goal, the money comes. Better yet, if that's the end goal, the meaning comes.

YOU ARE ONE OR THE OTHER

Artist or audience. You are one or the other. Each has a role to play in contributing to the best of who we are and what we hope to be.

AN APPEAL TO SPIRITUAL ARTISTS AND AUDIENCES

If your work is infused with your spirituality (and whose work is not?), your calling is clear: You are a co-creator, or re-creator of the master artist. You must make all things new by making new things. As Michelangelo reportedly wrote, "You must criticize by creating something beautiful." Your greatest contribution is to make the fullness of the earth more full.

The rest of us? We are the audience. There's the artist, then there is us. It's a connected relationship. We benefit one another.

Our call, as audiences, is equally clear: to make the best content profitable...yes, by giving our attention and dollars to the right things...and to popularize and to populate the best of human creation. Stop seeing yourself as a passive audience, or worse, a consumer. You are a patron, and maybe we start by simply ignoring the bad and finding the good. That's a good place to begin.

Our roles may be clear, but it's complicated, right? For both artist and audience. What to create? What not to create? How to make a living? How to impact the creative industries?

It's not easy—for the artist or for the audience.

I see myself in the story of Eutychus, a little known figure found in Scripture, who falls asleep listening to a late-night preacher...then comically falls out of the window. Maybe you're like me. I'm drifting off to sleep, even falling out of windows. I'm drowsy, fatigued and need someone and something to awaken me. The story itself may be thrilling—for the Christian, the story of a great rescue plan unfolding—but, our ways of telling it have become small and predictable. And audiences are drifting. This is where the artist must step in.

That does not mean—I repeat, that does not mean—creating more religious films or books or music or companies.

It's about, both, a deeper and more expansive view of God's story and our place in it. Being a servant-minded artist means exploring and expressing the full scope of the human experience.

There is much great learning from the Gospel story—even for the unbeliever. Jesus' story spans from the greatest evil in human history found at the splintered, blood-soaked Cross, where an innocent Man was killed, to the most glorious hope in history, the empty tomb, the scars of a Savior who did what He promised to do and awaits to rescue us all.

From the most horrific loss, to the most hopeful love, the Gospel speaks to all of life, does it not? How then, can we say to an artist not to explore the heights and depths of what it means to be human? As Dutch theologian Abraham Kuyper said, "There is not a square inch of all of creation where Christ does not say, 'Mine!'"

A baptized imagination does not limit artists to painting bowls of fruit or sugar plum cottages or wispy songs about heaven. It liberates the creative to build skyscrapers and Apple watches, write children's fiction and code for games that take us into new worlds.

Real things, designed and made beautifully, that contribute to the flourishing of our neighbors.

It makes sense, then, as we read in the Old Testament, that God would command blue pomegranates be sewn on the hem of the temple's priestly garments. There is no such thing as a blue pomegranate in nature.

It makes sense that author C.S. Lewis would write an exchange of letters between a senior and junior demon in *The Screwtape Letters*. A Christian writing in the voice of a demon? Absolutely.

So what does this mean for the artist and the audience? How far is too far? How narrow is too narrow? One thing is for sure. We still have not reached the edges. There is still a long way to go, and isn't it incredible that the ones who are giving us the most profound, most true, most honest and most beautiful explorations of the sacred are often those who don't have any motivation to do so? They are creators, simply creating.

That is why, first and foremost, we need to ask artists to tell the truth. To be honest. Not start with an agenda. Or be forced by funders to determine some return on investment of souls saved or elections won from their art.

Too many of our stories, especially in film, attempt to tell the entire story, leaving nothing to chance, without ambiguity or margins for interpretation. It's a total distrust of the audience and misuse of the arts.

Religious films, in particular, have many challenges. Most importantly, these films are riddled with theological problems—a flimsy understanding of what is good, true and beautiful. As a result, they have a problem that no expensive production or A-list actor can fix; the errors are embedded in the essence of the story from the very beginning.

The best art and entertainment raises questions, creates longing, offers delight that lasts long after the credits roll, the chapter ends, the gallery closes or the song fades. It haunts the audience.

Too many artists think they have to fix the world with their art—something called prescriptive truth—showing the world as it should be. I'm not entirely against that, but we need more descriptive truth—stories that show the world as it is—a diagnostic vision that provokes people to identify and to relate with what they see on the screen or on the page.

In the end, we must allow artists freedom and full access to create beautiful and lasting things with astonishing excellence.

MAKE THEM BETTER?

When George Frideric Handel wrote the *Messiah* in the summer of 1741, he spent three weeks in a locked room, refusing water and food, sprawled out on the floor, often weeping. He wrote 280 pages of music called the greatest work of music composition in history.

A servant peaked into his room and said, "I did think I saw heaven open, and saw the very face of God."

When he performed it before the royalty, they rose to their feet spontaneously during the Hallelujah chorus, a tradition that lasts to this day. When Lord Kimmel praised Handel for the fine entertainment, the composer responded, "Lord, I do not wish to simply entertain them; I wish to make them better."

How did he do it? By creating beauty that has stood the test of time, and, today, performed by choirs from colleges to churches to major city symphony halls all around the world.

CREATE AS IF NO ONE IS WATCHING

True artists create because they have to. They cannot help but do what they do. And, of course, we should be finding ways through grants, through scholarships, through commissions, through Kickstarter, through our daily consumption to support artists. That is the role of the audience.

The artist must remember that just because there is no audience, no applause, the work is no less important or meaningful.

Think of the Creator who makes fish that swim so deep no human or submarine camera could ever see; he makes flowers on mountaintops that bloom where no hiker or plane could ever find; he has set stars in galaxies that are so large they make ours look like a speck of dust, but even our best telescope will never reach.

Are they any less beautiful or worthy or significant? Not at all. As one singer-songwriter friend of mine said during a lengthy tour playing at bars and coffeehouses, "I play the same for five people as I do for 500 people. You never know who is listening."

IN DANGEROUS TIMES, DOES THE ARTIST MATTER?

A story goes that leaders from a war-torn country secretly gathered in a mountain village to prepare a list of their nation's most indispensable artists and thinkers. Their contributions to humanity, the leaders proposed, were too significant to risk their lives to the random tragedies found on the battlefield.

The invention of the light bulb and the car were bound to happen, the argument went, even if Edison and Ford had never lived. The artist, on the other hand, was unique. Lose an artist and you risk losing another Titian fresco, Beethoven's Fifth Symphony, or Shakespearean sonnet.

Lose an artist and their gifts are gone forever.

Here's the problem: The artist cannot be removed from the brokenness. The artist cannot play it safe or stay on the fringes. The artist must be the first into the mess, into the brokenness, into despair and hurt and pain and evil. That is their greatest service to us; to step in and serve a yard from hell. Offering signposts of hope and healing, to let imaginations fly beyond the stars, to provide delight and laughter, to pull back the veneer and reveal the life that really is.

THE 500-YEAR CREATIVE VISION

As artists, be fearless—love whatever is good and true and beautiful, use your calling with purpose, work for the common good, and do the unexpected. It's really that simple.

Create works so astonishing, so lasting, that in 50 or 100 or 500 years, future generations say: There, that one, that artist gave us a gift that awakened our hearts and minds and souls and didn't do it for money or fame, but did it all for those audiences to come.

HERE LIVED A GREAT STREET SWEEPER

"If a man is called to be a street sweeper, he should sweep streets even as Michelangelo painted, or Beethoven composed music or Shakespeare wrote poetry. He should sweep streets so well that all the hosts of heaven and earth will pause to say, 'Here lived a great street sweeper who did his job well.'"

– Dr. Martin Luther King

—

NOT ALL WHO WANDER ARE LOST.

—

LOVE THE THINGS YOU CAN CONTROL

Learn to love the process, not the outcome. You can control how you do things. You cannot control whether the final result is a success or not.

THE "IN-BETWEENERS"

"The middle space" is that beautiful and mysterious tension between art and commerce, audience and content, what is and what could be. It's where honesty meets aspiration. Where we tell better stories that ask deeper questions, create more real conversations and leave larger margins for people to come to their own conclusions in their own time. The content we produce. The content we promote. It's all designed for those "in-betweeners" who have a hard-time defining who they are or what they believe, but they know it when they are with others, or when they see it on the screen, or read it on the page, or hear it on their playlist. It's a desire for what is real, true and, once experienced, makes you uneasy and unsatisfied with what lies on either side—the mass-marketed glossiness on one side and the dull predictability on the other. If you believe in the "the middle space" or find your home there in the messiness, welcome.

WATCH HIS EYES

You need not see what someone is doing to know if it is his vocation, you have only to watch his eyes; a cook mixing a sauce, a surgeon making a primary incision, a clerk completing a bill of lading, wear the same rapt expression, forgetting themselves in a function. How beautiful it is, that eye-on-the-object look.

– W. H. Auden

—

VOCATIONS DON'T TAKE VACATIONS.

—

RICHEST MAN IN THE CEMETERY

"Being the richest man in the cemetery doesn't matter to me. Going to bed at night saying we've done something wonderful, that's what matters to me."

– Steve Jobs

—

LIFESTYLES OF THE POOR AND UNKNOWN ARE FAR MORE FASCINATING THAN LIFESTYLES OF THE RICH AND FAMOUS.

—

RADICAL IS NOT A BAD WORD

Radical religious belief is not wrong and dangerous. Radical wrong religious belief is dangerous.

Consider this:

Radical following of Jesus would mean relentless love, serving a yard from hell to help those in need, defending the orphan and widow, extreme humility, befriending the stranger, unimaginable generosity, loving your enemy, thankfulness in all circumstances, joy in suffering, and seeking forgiveness every chance you can.

IN US WE TRUST

If you're a millennial, you've learned that you can't trust your parents. You can't trust the politicians. You can't trust the police. You can't trust the courts. You can't trust the banks. You can't trust the media. You can't trust your friends. You can't trust your boyfriend. You can't trust your school. You can't trust the stranger. You can't trust your neighbor. You can't trust your teachers. Trust is essential to a democracy, to law, to education, to neighborhoods, to marriages, to friendships, to leadership...it's all on us to rebuild it.

—

WHEN TRUTH AND GOODNESS FADE, TRY BEAUTY.

—

ALL THINGS IN ABUNDANCE

We implicitly appreciate common grace in areas of our lives—we compliment our neighbor on her garden, we feast upon a great meal at our favorite restaurant, and we cheer the speed and power of an Olympic swimmer.

We delight in things made by those who don't share our spirituality, as we should.

We don't ask if our surgeon is religious—we just want the best one at the hospital.

We don't ask a landscaper for an estimate and for their theology before they start laying sod.

And, yet, in the creative spheres, for some reason we are so reluctant—even restrained—to see goodness, truth and beauty in others.

We should praise the musical *Hamilton*, films like *Calvary* and *St. Vincent*, songs from Arcade Fire and Ingrid Michaelson—and while these works are not perfect or pure in their theology *or* their expression—they do carry profound insights into the human condition.

Wherever there is truth. Wherever there is beauty. Wherever there is goodness. That is where we should be. We should be in the audience, rising to our feet, giving it a standing ovation, calling out for an encore.

LEAVE IT BETTER

My dad taught me that when you borrow something you always return it better than how you found it. Like when a friend lets you borrow a car. You always wash it and fill it up before returning. Same is true with our role in society. We are on borrowed time, borrowed resources, borrowed gifts. We should return society better than when we first found it.

WHO WILL STEP FORWARD?

Everyone agrees we need a smarter, more civil, more thoughtful and high-minded social conversation—that conversation cannot be led by people who care about status or wealth or ratings or power or hanging onto stale ideologies.

—

IS YOUR BUSINESS PLAYING TO WIN OR PLAYING NOT TO LOSE? THERE'S A BIG DIFFERENCE.

—

"...OUR MOST POWERFUL STORYTELLERS ARE NO LONGER SHAMANS, PRIESTS, PRESIDENTS, OR GENERALS...TODAY'S STORYTELLERS ARE [IN COMPANIES]."

—WINNING THE STORY WARS, BY JONAH SACHS

RULED BY BUFFOONS

"I am conscious of having been ruled by buffoons, taught by idiots, preached at by hypocrites, and preyed upon by charlatans in the guise of advertisers and other professional persuaders, as well as by demagogues and ideologues of many opinions, all false."

– Malcolm Muggeridge.

WHEN YOU DON'T KNOW WHERE YOU'RE HEADED, YOU GO BACKWARDS.

SELL THE SOLUTION

Is your company solving a problem? Many companies are selling their innovation or their experience or their leadership or their pricing. The best companies are selling a solution to a problem.

FLAIR

"[Audiences]...want popular music and stories that are fun and entertaining, artistically good and sometimes innovative, but that are also concerned with addressing the issues of life with artistic flair."

– William Romanowski, author and professor

THAT'S GREAT

Be careful using the word "great" before any creative work. Great film. Great book. Great music. It's been so overused, it's become meaningless. Give something 50 or 500 years to marinate and to cure before you call it great.

"Art is never finished, only abandoned."

– Leonardo da Vinci

THE DRUG OF AN ENTREPRENEUR

Is there anything more magical than when an atom of an idea begins to crackle and spark and others begin to say, "I want that"?

The fastest way to learn your weaknesses is to become an entrepreneur.

MORNING PEOPLE

There's a reason entrepreneurs love the morning more than the night. They rise from their beds believing that anything can happen. At night, they fall to sleep knowing some things never did.

FINDING YOUR FLOW

Surround yourself with people who are smarter and better than you. We need to learn that we're not good at thousands of things, and pretty good at two or three. Start doing those few things now and leave the rest to others.

—

PONDER ANEW.

—

THE MYSTERY

The best artists begin without the end in mind; it's about finding the story within the paint, the prose, the marble, the idea.

THE GENEROUS CREATIVE

To hoard or not to hoard? It's a big challenge for those in business when it comes to ideas, contacts and opportunities. It's super subversive and counter-intuitive to be generous with such things. It only makes sense if you believe that it's not all about you, and you have a vision for something bigger than collecting titles or pay stubs. I have seen people take my ideas. I've seen people cut and paste my proposal for their own pitches. You have two choices: be better or be bitter. And believe me, it's much easier to live with hands unclenched. Not there yet, but getting closer everyday.

—

BLESSED ARE THE WEIRD PEOPLE.

—

A PECULIAR PEOPLE

We need people who long to walk the streets, not the red carpets; cling to authenticity, not to awards. People who admire the poor and unknown, not the rich and famous. Creatives who make haunting work—work that leaves the audience a little better off than they were when they first picked up the book or magazine, entered the theater or gallery, turned on the television or the Spotify playlist.

—

STAY DIFFERENT. STAY WEIRD. BE A PECULIAR PEOPLE. IT'S A SIGN OF THE HOPE OF GLORY WITHIN YOU.

—

THREE ESSENTIALS

Entrepreneurship comes down to putting these three things together: what you're best at, what you're most passionate about, and what has the best chance of making money. Just having two of the three, any two, is not sustainable.

YOU'RE NOT MADE TO DABBLE

The primary call of your life is not convenience and comfort or finding the right spouse, walking red carpets or earning prestigious honors and awards, getting the right job or electing the right people to Congress. It is not even to change the world. Dabbling. Tinkering. Standing back. Pinching pennies. Waiting your turn. Dipping in your toe. Your call is far more profound, more glorious than that. As a creative, you were made to be a pioneer not a settler. No maps. No compass. No month of provisions. Just aspirations that you feel deep in your gut that cannot be easily explained or justified, let alone derailed.

PAINTING THE BACKS OF DRAWERS

Why did Walt Disney make sure that even the stuff you'd never see at Disneyland be done with excellence? Why does a great furniture maker paint the backs of drawers? Why were the never-to-be-seen undergarments of the costumes in *Braveheart* authentic to the era? Why do flowers bloom on mountaintops that will never be seen by humans? Because the creator knows. And art isn't just what's seen, but also what's unseen. It's for the artist even more than the audience.

DON'T
FEAR
MONEY

Here's my challenge: Cast your fears aside. Your reputation should only really matter to those who love and know you. Ignore everyone else. Do your thing. And, don't fear money. It comes and goes. Live free from that ridiculous trap. And pride? Take pride in your passions not your position or paycheck. You've been given the greatest gift anyone could have: the chance to wake up and chase your dreams. Be thankful. Most people never get that chance.

—
"WE WIN OR WE LEARN."
— INGLE MARTIN, FOOTBALL COACH
—

FAIL OFTEN

Fail, retool, pivot, try again. Do it as many times as you can. Don't believe the naysayers that see failure as a sign of weakness. It's a sign of a daring spirit, the stuff that every great entrepreneur and innovator and designer and artist goes through to reach greatness. I think I've failed at least a dozen times in the past two years on ideas and initiatives. I'm proud of each and every one because the failures refine, sharpen and move me forward. Don't rest on success. Fail as often as you can.

—
SHOW YOUR CREATIVE WORK TO STRANGERS.
FRIENDS AND FAMILY ARE NEVER HONEST.
—

THE TEMPTATIONS

I'm tempted to move, so I'll be still. I'm tempted to be complicated, so I'll be simple. I'm tempted to be loud, so I'll be silent. I'm tempted to be profane, so I'll be sacred. I'm tempted to be fast, so I'll be slow. I'm tempted to be big, so I'll be small. I'm tempted to be first, so I'll be last. I'm tempted to be greedy, so I'll be generous. I'm tempted to be known, so I'll serve.

—

MAKE GOODNESS FASHIONABLE.

—

JOIN THE INDEPENDENCE PARTY

The older I get, the more independent I become—who I vote for, what I watch, what I listen to, where I shop, who I hang out with. Yes, it's a reaction to having a 10th-row center seat in politics and entertainment and institutions. But it's more than that. It's my belief that independence creates more dependency on my Creator and more inter-dependence with my neighbor.

THE STRUGGLE WE SHARE

Every morning, I pray away the demons, rise, step into The Struggle, wrestle it to the ground, often walking away limping, but always believing that the beauty of business is not the success but the process. It's the messy middle where you find the life that is really life. Ask any successful businessman or woman: Their fondest memories are the early years. The scrappiness. The possibilities. The Struggle.

—

THERE ARE WELL-TOLD LIES. THERE ARE POORLY-TOLD TRUTHS. HOW ABOUT CREATING MORE WELL-TOLD TRUTHS?

—

THERE IS NO PLAYBOOK

There is joy in meeting creatives who tear up the playbook and ask, "Is there a better way to do this?" Conversely, there is pain in meeting creatives who will sacrifice their own aspirations for a chance of a record or film or publishing deal.

SLEEP
BETTER

"There are two kinds of people in the world: givers and takers. The takers may eat better, but the givers sleep better."

– Performer Danny Thomas

THE GETTING IS IN THE GIVING

Pray not that you will get more, but that you will give more.

GIVING IT AWAY

The sign of creative vitality is not how much you are making, but how much you are giving. Be generous in your work.

WARMING THE BENCH

Can you hear the songs of the lonely? Do you see the stories of the heartbroken? Are you reading the longings of rich and poor? They are everywhere, for those who have ears to hear and eyes to see. Where are we? Are we close enough to listen? Are we near enough to see it up close and personal? Or are we a bystander? Outside the arena? Safe and secluded?

Shake off the dust, friends, It's time to step in, move toward, go farther, stoop low, slow down, and love the hell out of the world.

PLAYFULNESS

G.K. Chesterton said, "If a thing is worth doing, it's worth doing badly." We are such serious people. Play and leisure—a day at the ballpark, good food and wine with friends, painting and ballroom dancing—things worth doing whether the team loses, the food burns, the paint drips, the feet trip—joy in the playing without perfection or pressure. Healthy creativity includes joyful play. Lots of it.

THE LANGUAGE OF ASPIRATION

If you've ever said, "I bet we could...Why don't we...I believe...What if...If only...Can you imagine...How about...I wonder...This could be better...I wish...What do you think...When will that..." Well, then you were saying and showing what it means to be aspirational. Inspiration appreciates good things. Aspiration makes them happen.

BULLETS, THEN CANNONBALLS

Jim Collins, in *Great by Choice,* describes "bullets, then cannonballs," where you fire small bullets to see what works and what doesn't, and then, once the model is proven, you fire cannonballs. Bullets don't sink ships— cannonballs can. In this current economy, firing bullets to calibrate your aim and your opportunity is very smart.

DRIP VS. DOWNPOUR

Be careful when celebrating "cloudburst" moments, that is, when victories are big and significant. When down pours come hard and fast, what happens? People run for shelter and important things erode. It is far more powerful to pursue the droplet strategy...drip...drip...drip... Lasting, meaningful good comes from patient, persistent work over years, decades and centuries. So, your movie or book or song hit big on the charts? So, your candidate or cause won? Wonderful, but did it create the deep grooves that direct the course of human events?

WHEN THEY LAUGH
AT YOU

First, they ignore you. Then, they laugh at you. Then, fight you. Eventually, they try to compete with you. If you are not at one of these stages right now with your business or product, then you are playing the same game as everyone else, and it's time to start looking around your industry and ask, "What can be done better?"

S IS FOR...

Smallness.
Stillness.
Simplicity.
Stability.
Sabbath.
Sacrifice.
Service.
Solitude.
Slowness.
Subversive.

THE MIDDLE VS. THE CENTER

Our call is to be in the middle, not in the center. The middle of life, industries, conversations, conflict and so on. The middle is messy, unsafe. The center, well, is self-centered and quite safe as it puts you—and not others—as the reference point.

HAUNTING YOUR AUDIENCE

After the credits roll...the song ends...the last page is turned...the gallery closes—the greatest accomplishment of art is to "haunt" the audience. To linger in your audience: glory. To be forgotten: hell.

THE FOUR ELEMENTS OF GREAT ART

Heart, soul, mind and strength. The essentials for the creation of great art. Leave out heart, and you have no emotion. Leave out mind, and you risk hyper-sentimentalism. Leave out soul, and you have no transcendence. Leave out strength, and you have no struggle.

THE EARLY RISER

Here's to the early risers. The ones we take for granted and rarely see—stocking the shelves, grinding the coffee, turning on the lights, delivering the goods—all before we wake. While it's still cold and dark, they are setting the city in motion. Their days start earlier and end later. Our days are easier because of what they do. Make their invisible work more visible today by saying, "Thanks." You'll just need to get up earlier to do it.

GRIT

A University of Pennsylvania study says that GRIT is more valuable than talent in business... "You need employees with stamina and tenacity above all else." From personal experience, this is absolutely true. Take grit over whit, tenacity over talent, stamina over strategy any day.

LEBRON JAMES IS 10 FEET AWAY

Do you ever feel like the arena security guard who sits with his or her back to the court, so close to the action but forced to stare at the cheering crowd? We've all felt that way at one time or another. We couldn't be any closer, but we couldn't be any more removed from what's going on.

RULES WORTH FOLLOWING

Validation and success. These drive so much bizarre behavior. The need to be on the bestseller's list, number one at the box office, topping the charts. Strong enough to cause people to do anything to get there. Rigging the system. Stacking the deck. And, maybe not surprising, it is often done by those who are supposed to be living by a different standard. A different drummer lives and works and thinks and plays by a different set of rules, but there are still some rules worth following.

YOU'LL MAKE MORE MONEY SAYING, "NO"

Good work for good clients leads to more good clients. Good work for bad clients leads to more bad clients. Bad work for good clients leads to no more clients. Don't ever be afraid to say "no!"

BE RECKLESS

The cure for greed is reckless generosity.

—

"WE USED TO PRAISE ART; NOW WE PRAISE CASH."

—BOB LEFSETZ, THE LEFSETZ LETTER

—

RELAX. IT'S GOING TO BE OK.

One of the lessons every entrepreneur needs to learn:
Walk in the unforced rhythms of grace.
Right? Easier said than done.

> We sprint.
> We force.
> We are erratic.
> We are willful.

When we walk without forcing our way. In a steady rhythm. In grace. That is a beautiful thing.

TWO EARS. ONE MOUTH.

The art of persuasion is dying. In response, we talk more and louder and harder. Want to know how to persuade people? Listen more and longer and harder. Then tell stories and use humor. Everything else is white noise.

—

JUST BECAUSE SOMETHING IS POSSIBLE DOESN'T MEAN IT'S PROFITABLE.

—

MONEY IS MANURE

It's rightly said that money is like manure; pile it up and it starts to stink, but spread it around and watch things grow.

MORE CHLORINE NEEDED

So much of "American culture" is similar to a two-star hotel hot tub. How do you fix that? Some argue we should drain it. Others get out and avoid it altogether. A few want to build an alternative. Far too many want to just turn on the jets and lounge in it. What do you think?

"A" FOR EFFORT

We should applaud excellence and experience, not good
intentions and effort.

SHOW ME THE WAY

"You don't always have to chop with the sword of truth.
You can point with it, too."

–Anne Lamott in *Bird by Bird*

BIGGER AIN'T BETTER

We love big, don't we? We think that's the measure of success and significance. And yet that goes against the reality
that the most meaningful things in life are in the small—
in business, relationships, art, kids, government, faith. It's
when we get low, stoop, pause and, in fact, decrease, that
things really happen.

THE GREATEST MOMENT

We are living in the greatest moment in the history of modern storytelling—as creators and as consumers.

THE EARTHSHAKING DRAMA

Where are those artists who are creating an "earthshaking drama where angels peer expectantly over their human shoulders to see what is coming out of the palette or typewriter next" as author Calvin Seerveld wrote?

SAFE AIN'T SANE

Enough with the melodramas. Abandon middle road mediocrity. Rip "safe" from your vocabulary. Artists, we need you to be daring.

RISK BIG

"In many ways the life of the critic is easy. We risk very little, yet, enjoy the position over those who offer up their work and their selves to judgment. We thrive on negative criticism, which is fun to write and to read. But, the bitter truth we critics must face is that, in the grand scheme of things, the average piece of junk is probably more meaningful than our criticism designating it so. But, there are times when a critic truly risks something, and that is in the discovery and defense of the new. The world is often unkind to new talent, new creations. The new needs friends."

– Anton Ego, the food critic in the movie, *Ratatouille*

CONTENTMENT

If you were last, would that be okay? When everyone is rising and thriving, would you be okay? If your friends and your enemies were richer and smarter, would it be okay? When those around you are getting a break, seeing their dreams realized, would you still be okay? If it never happened for you, all those dreams and all those hopes, would you, really, be okay?

Nothing is more beautiful than a contented soul.

THE FINISH LINE

The number one hardest lesson to learn in business—if you are a starter, a conceiver, a finder—is to be a finisher. Young entrepreneurs, learn that lesson as soon as you can.

—

THERE'S NEVER A BAD TIME TO SAY, "I WAS WRONG." THERE'S NEVER A GOOD TIME TO SAY, "I WAS RIGHT."

—

A FINAL WORD

In 2011 at the Sunshine Theater in New York City, about 350 people of various beliefs and backgrounds gathered to screen the Fox Searchlight film, *The Tree of Life*. As we marketed the movie, some audiences would walk out of the theater, angry and confused. Others were so moved that they couldn't move, weeping in their seats. It was clear that this film was raising big questions and starting long conversations.

We had brought panelists to speak after the screening—a top humanist, a Buddhist monk, the head of American Atheists, the head of the American Bible Society, a modern painter, a producer, and a pastor from Trinity Wall Street Church.

The Fox Searchlight executives stood in the back of the auditorium, their social media teams ready to tweet out quotes to followers.

The atheist started the panel with no holds barred, "This is a Christian movie. No question in mind."

Down the line they went, offering their interpretation: This is no movie; it's a prayer, a cathedral, a meditation—anything but a movie.

The executive from the American Bible Society said, "This movie is like a bomb going off in a Crayola Crayon factory; it's a big beautiful mess."

The painter, Makoto Fujimura, said, "Christ came not to make us Christian, but to make us more human."

Meanwhile, Fox Searchlight's Twitter feed was lighting up with these quotes.

I thought to myself: Does it get any better than this? That moment in Sunshine Theater was more holy and more sacred than most Sunday morning church services.

The most sacred places can be made secular, the most secular places can be made sacred.

In that sacred moment, an audience of strangers bound together in a shared experience.

It was an artistic work that explored the ease of grace and the force of human will.

A panel of various beliefs, all agreeing that this a religious experience, disturbing for some, divine for others. And a major entertainment company populating their feeds with quotes about art, faith, beauty, grace.

That is common grace...that is art for the common good on display.

An honest entertainment executive would tell you: The best stories, the most imaginative filmmakers are not found in Hollywood. They are in places like Wilmore or Wilmington or Walla Walla.

We are seeing a great democratization of Hollywood. Little "Hollywoods" will spring up everywhere. What a good thing! History has shown that the people and the places that typically change the world are those we least expect.

No doubt you sense my urgency to see artists and audiences, creatives and consumers to rise above the mindless and mediocre and mundane. To live in the middle. To deepen our stories. To be generous in our collaboration. To be rooted in the things that matter most.

My greatest hope for us all:

That we would let our imagination fly beyond the stars, as Francis Schaeffer wrote; that we would go deeper and farther than we ever thought we could, as our story is infinitely dimensional—drawn from the most horrific act to the most beautiful act in history; that we would love common grace; that we would never bow to celebrity or money or expectations; that we would put truth and grace to story and song and symbols in ways no one else can; that we would welcome the peculiar; that we would embrace the struggle and the war within; that we would be prayerful and sacramental; that we would be originators not imitators; and that we would know—truly know—that all of us are needed and loved and wanted far more than any words can possibly express.

ERIK LOKKESMOE

Co-founder and principal of Different Drummer, Erik Lokkesmoe has more than 20 years of experience in architecting and executing media campaigns within the corporate, government, and entertainment sectors. His professional career includes Capitol Hill press secretary, Cabinet-level and celebrity speechwriter, head of communications for the national endowment, manager at the National Association of Broadcasters, and VP of strategic partnerships for the Anschutz Film Group and Walden Media. Erik has co-authored two books and received a M.A. in Public Communication with an emphasis in Social Marketing.

elevate
publishing

**DELIVERING TRANSFORMATIVE MESSAGES
TO THE WORLD**

Visit www.elevatepub.com for our latest offerings.

NO TREES WERE HARMED IN THE MAKING OF THIS BOOK.

OK, so a few did make the ultimate sacrifice.

In order to steward our environment, we are partnered with *Plant With Purpose*, to plant a tree for every tree that paid the price for the printing of this book.

To learn more, visit www.elevatepub.com/about